Decomposers

by Grace Hansen

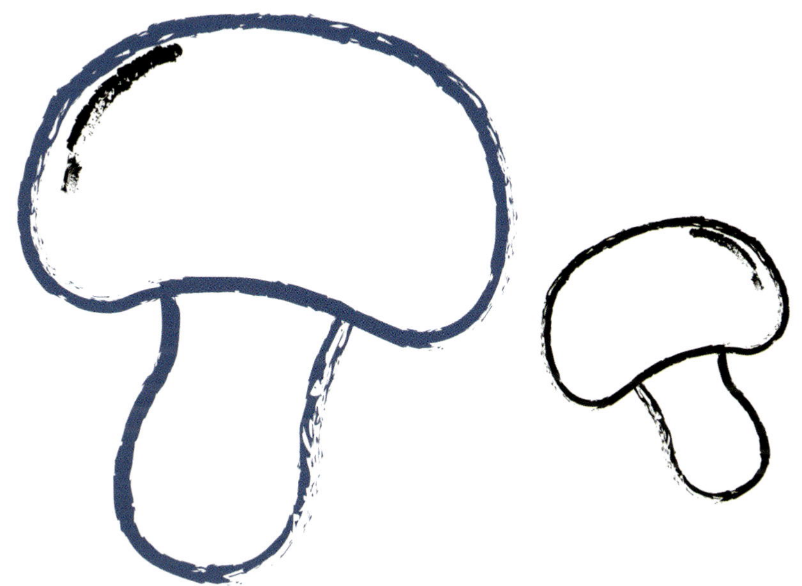

abdobooks.com

Published by Abdo Kids, a division of ABDO, P.O. Box 398166, Minneapolis, Minnesota 55439.
Copyright © 2020 by Abdo Consulting Group, Inc. International copyrights reserved in all countries.
No part of this book may be reproduced in any form without written permission from the publisher.
Abdo Kids Jumbo™ is a trademark and logo of Abdo Kids.

Printed in the United States of America, North Mankato, Minnesota.

102019

012020

THIS BOOK CONTAINS
RECYCLED MATERIALS

Photo Credits: iStock, Shutterstock

Production Contributors: Teddy Borth, Jennie Forsberg, Grace Hansen
Design Contributors: Dorothy Toth, Pakou Moua

Library of Congress Control Number: 2019941221

Publisher's Cataloging-in-Publication Data

Names: Hansen, Grace, author.

Title: Decomposers / by Grace Hansen

Description: Minneapolis, Minnesota : Abdo Kids, 2020 | Series: Beginning science: ecology |
    Includes online resources and index.

Identifiers: ISBN 9781532188930 (lib. bdg.) | ISBN 9781644942666 (pbk.) |
    ISBN 9781532189425 (ebook) | ISBN 9781098200404 (Read-to-Me ebook)

Subjects: LCSH: Decomposition (Biology)--Juvenile literature. | Biodegradation--Juvenile literature. | Food
    webs (Ecology)--Juvenile literature. | Ecology--Juvenile literature. | Resource recovery--Juvenile
    literature.

Classification: DDC 577.16--dc23

Table of Contents

What Are Decomposers?

Decomposers are an important part of the food chain.

4

Food chains show how energy
flows through an **ecosystem**.
Decomposers show up in the
chain when there is **waste**.

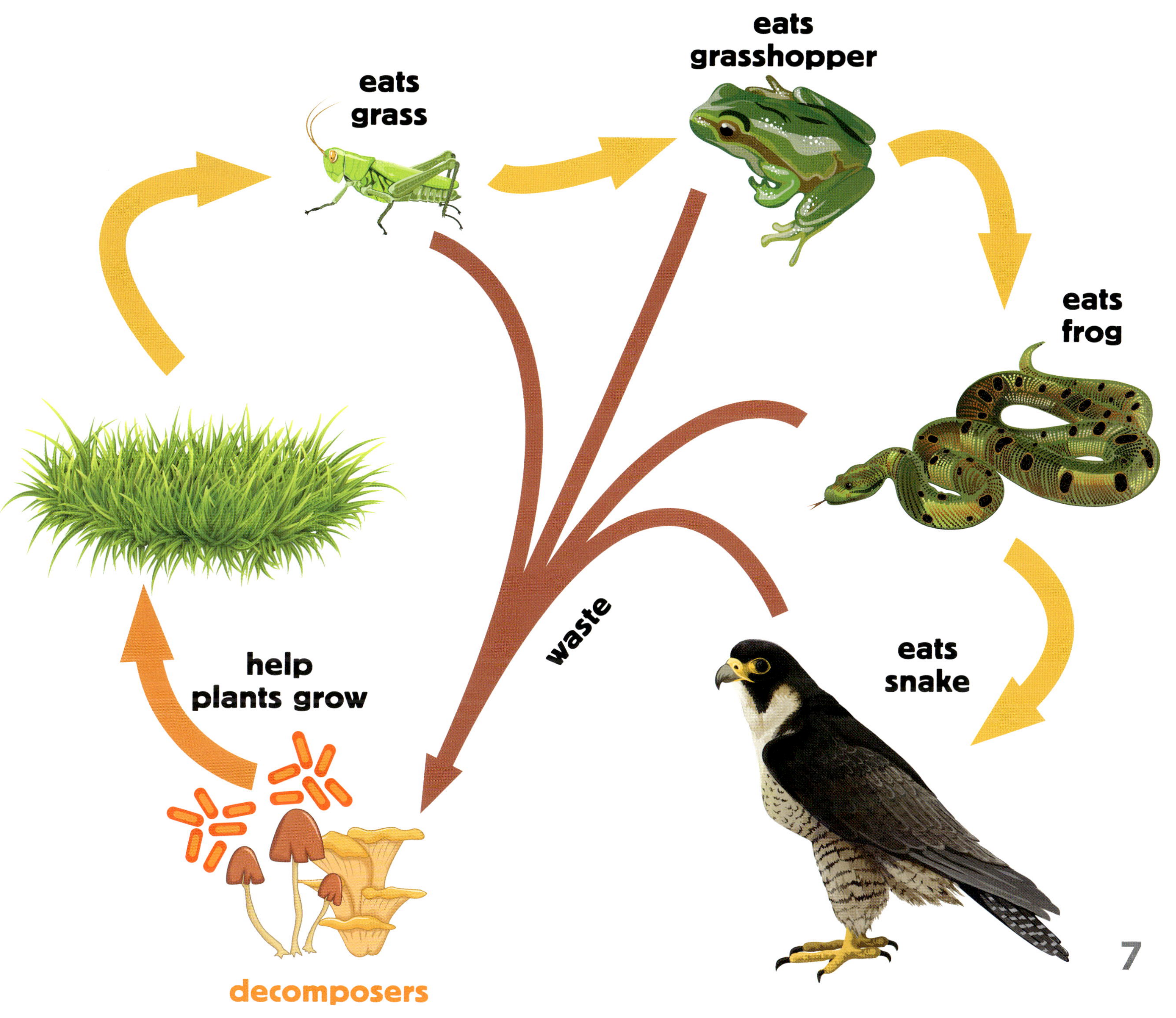

eats
grass
eats
grasshopper
eats
frog
eats
snake
waste
help
plants grow
decomposers
7

Decomposers keep **waste** from building up in an **ecosystem**.

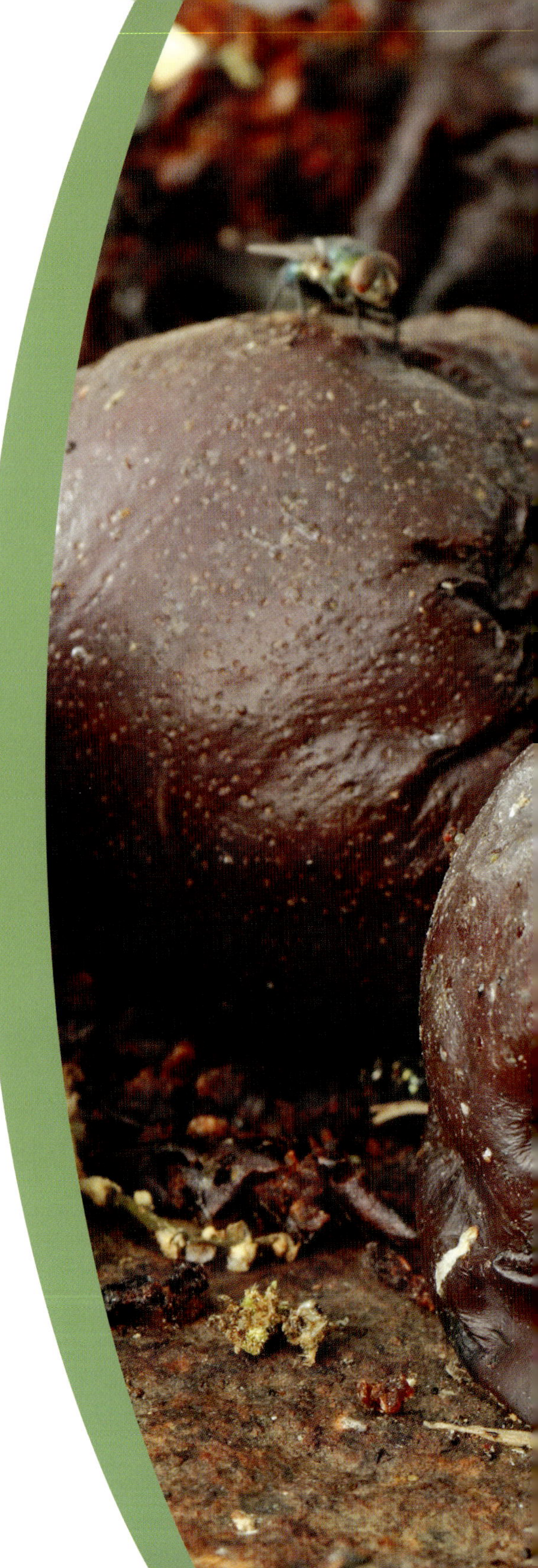

9

Waste comes in many forms. It can be leaves that have fallen from trees. It can be animal droppings.

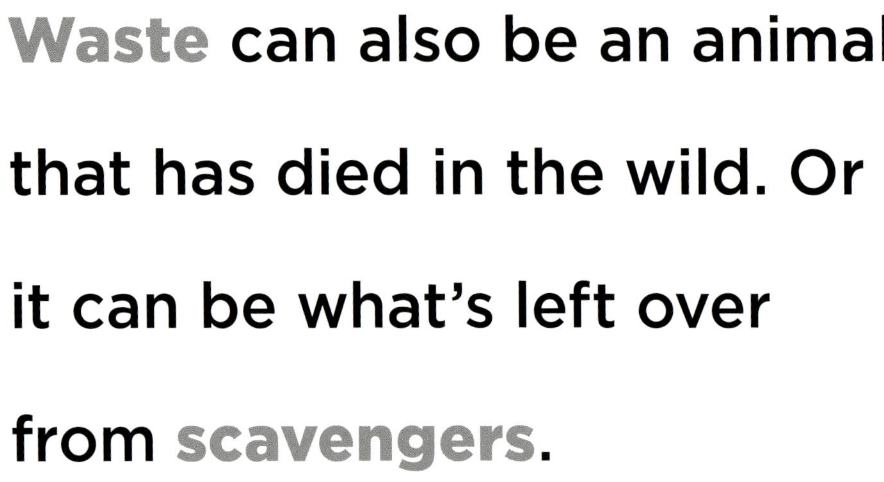

Waste can also be an animal that has died in the wild. Or it can be what's left over from **scavengers**.

Bacteria & Fungi

You need a **microscope** to see some decomposers. Bacteria are very small. But they help break down an animal's dead body.

bacteria

Fungi can be seen without
a **microscope**. They release
special **enzymes**. These
enzymes help break down
dead plants and animals.

Certain types of fungi like to decompose fruits and vegetables.

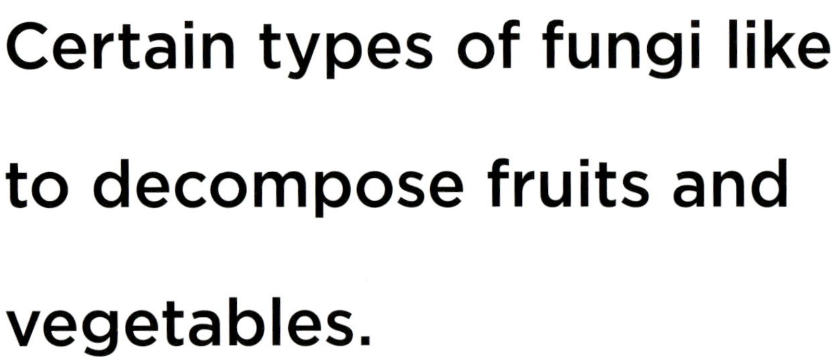

19

All decomposers break down

waste into tiny chemical parts.

These chemicals are put back

into the soil. This helps plants

grow.

Let's Review!

- Decomposers put nutrients back into the soil. This helps plants grow.

- Without them, Earth would be full of waste.

- Scavengers break down large pieces of organic material, like dead animals, by eating them.

- Decomposers break down dead, organic matter. This can happen after a scavenger is done with it.

- Detritivores eat dead, organic matter. Unlike bacteria and fungi, they digest it internally to gain nutrients. Earthworms are an example.

Glossary

ecosystem – a community of livings things, together with their environment.

enzyme – a protein that helps a chemical reaction take place within a living thing.

microscope – an instrument that uses a lens to make very small objects larger so that they can be seen by the eye.

scavenger – animals that break down large pieces of organic material, like dead animals, by eating them.

waste – a dead plant or animal or the droppings of animals.

Index

Visit **abdokids.com** to access crafts, games, videos, and more!